Mr. Greg's Garden

Ari Brennan
Illustrated by Pat Reynolds

Mr. Greg planted a garden.
He planted bean seeds.

The bean seeds grew into bean plants.

Rabbits came to the garden.
They ate the leaves of the bean plants.

So Mr. Greg made a fence.

Deer came to the garden.

They ate the stems of the bean plants.

So Mr. Greg made some noise.

Birds came to the garden.

They ate the beans on the bean plants.

So Mr. Greg made a scarecrow.

Rabbits, deer, and birds
came to the garden.
They ate more bean plants!

Mr. Greg had an idea.

He planted a new garden.

He fixed his old garden.

Mr. Greg picked his beans.
He ate them for lunch.

14

The animals ate their plants, too!